Decodable Stories

Grade 2
Book 2

Bothell, WA • Chicago, IL • Columbus, OH • New York, NY

MHEonline.com

Copyright © 2015 McGraw-Hill Education

All rights reserved. No part of this publication may be reproduced or distributed in any form or by any means, or stored in a database or retrieval system, without the prior written consent of McGraw-Hill Education, including, but not limited to, network storage or transmission, or broadcast for distance learning.

Send all inquiries to:
McGraw-Hill Education
8787 Orion Place
Columbus, OH 43240

ISBN: 978-0-07-679723-3
MHID: 0-07-679723-6

Printed in the United States of America.

5 6 7 8 9 LON 24 23 22

Table of Contents

10 Chips 1
11 The Red Star 9
12 A Bridge 17
13 A Lunch List 25
14 No Drinks in Class 33
15 Paddle, Duck, Paddle 41
16 Learning to Swim 49
17 Farm Chores 57
18 Tracks at a Pond 65

Decodable Stories' Table 72

Chips

by Chester Shipley
illustrated by C. A. Nobens

Decodable Story 10

Upon a shelf sits a dish of chips. Seth is a big chips fan. Is that shelf too far up?

Seth sets a box upon a bench. Could that box get Seth far up?

Seth is still an inch away! Seth sets a thin rug upon the box.

With the thin rug, Seth can just brush his hand on the dish. Seth still cannot get that dish.

"I wish I could get chips! I will jump!" yells Seth. Then Seth did jump. Crash! Seth hit the shelf!

Crash! The dish and chips hit Seth! But Seth is glad. He grabs chips to munch!

The Red Star

by Lynn Frankel
illustrated by Judy Nostrandt

Decodable Story 11

Bothell, WA • Chicago, IL • Columbus, OH • New York, NY

Mark, Chad, and Trish sit in a park. Mark calls out, "This is not much fun in the dark."

"Let's wish upon a star!" Chad grins.
"Which star?" asks Trish.
"Start with that red star!" yells Chad.

"I will start," calls Chad. "I wish to be rich. I want as much cash as I can get!"

Then Trish is next. "I want a fast car. When I want to, I can zip to far off lands!"

13

"For which do you wish?" Chad asks Mark. "Cash? Cars?"

Mark kids Chad, "I wish you were smart."
Chad yells, "I am smart!"
Mark grins, "But you just wished upon Mars, not a star!"

A Bridge

by Gretchen Decker
illustrated by Paul Meisel

Decodable Story 12

Bothell, WA • Chicago, IL • Columbus, OH • New York, NY

This bridge is big! Jack's class will walk over it and back.

Cars and trucks go past. Jack never looks at traffic. Jack looks at this big bridge! Jack spots a patch of mist.

Jack stands at the bridge's edge. Jack can see dark water in spots.

Then Jack spots a big ship. Can it pass under this bridge? It will never fit. Will it hit this bridge? It will scratch it!

But that ship can fit under the bridge. How can they pack such big stacks on it?

That big ship will go to a dock. Jack would like to visit that dock!

A Lunch List

by Dennis Fertig
illustrated by Merrill Rainey

Decodable Story 13

Jess had to get eight lunches for eight pals. Plus Jess had to get lunch, too. Jess had to get nine lunches.

Jess grabbed a pen and printed a list. Eight lunches had to have sandwiches. Jess's lunch had to have a sandwich.

Jess had to get nine cups for water. Jess had to get napkins and dishes.

Jess checked her list. Jess asked Mack to check it. Mack said, "This list is good!"

Jess slipped on dark sunglasses. "I will fetch lunch and be back fast," Jess yelled to Mack.

As Jess jogged to a lunch truck, Mack spotted Jess's list on his desk. Mack grinned. "Jess will get back very fast," Mack said.

No Drinks in Class

by Luke Fisher
illustrated by John Edwards

Decodable Story 14

It is the end of May. Our class is hot. It is hard to think.

Bring me a bucket of water. I will splash and have fun.

Pick a dock, and I will jump off it. I will not sink.

If I were king, I'd sing, "Bring things to drink. Bring six pink drinks!"

I beg, but Mrs. Bridges will not budge.
She tells me, "No drinks in class!"

I am stuck in this hot class. I am sweating and sticking to my desk. "This stinks!" I think.

When the bell rings, I start singing. Thank you bell! Thanks, Mrs. Bridges!

Paddle, Duck, Paddle

by Eileen Breeze
illustrated by Stephanie Pershing

Decodable Story 15

Mc Graw Hill Education

Bothell, WA • Chicago, IL • Columbus, OH • New York, NY

Hank is a little duck. He zings past a puddle and gravel.

"I will get a snack," Hank thinks.

"I want bread. That's why I will use my head to get bread!"

Hank paddles to the middle of the pond and spots seven girls picknicking on the bank.

"Why, I think they will have bread!"

"I must use these strong legs to paddle!" Hank puffs. "I'm traveling as fast as I can."

Hank quacks, flapping his wings.
"Look, a little duck!" giggles one of the seven.
"I think little ducks like to gobble bread!"

The girl fumbles and tosses bread to Hank.
Hank gobbles it up and quacks, "Thank you!"

Learning to Swim

by Eileen Breeze
illustrated by John Edwards

Decodable Story 16

Mc Graw Hill Education

Bothell, WA • Chicago, IL • Columbus, OH • New York, NY

"When can I learn to swim, Dad?" asks Burt.
"Let's start after lunch," Dad tells Burt.

After lunch, Dad helps Burt learn to swim.
"Dad, will I get hurt in the water?"
"I will never let you get hurt, Burt."

First, Burt puts his legs under the water.
Then his arms are under the water!

Burt is swimming a little better.
"Dad, may I jump in the water?" Burt asks.
"Yes!" grins Dad.

First, Burt stands up. Then Burt jumps!
Burt's head is under the water!

"Dad, I have never had this much fun!" yells Burt. "And I can still learn to swim much better!"

Farm Chores

**by Edward Bricker
illustrated by Karen Tafoya**

Decodable Story 17

Bothell, WA • Chicago, IL • Columbus, OH • New York, NY

Dora is a farmer. In the morning she gets up in the dark to do her chores.

"I wish I did not have chores," she thinks. "But I like to be with the animals."

"I wish upon that star!" Dora thinks, "No chores!"

Dora brings water for the animals.
"I still have more chores!" Dora mutters. "I must ride the black horse to the store."

Dora sits on her horse. "Run fast!" The horse jumps. "Faster! Faster!" Dora yells. "We must be quick or we will miss the sun getting up!"

62

Dora grins. Here is the sun!
"I wish one more thing. I wish all days were just like this!"

Tracks at a Pond

by Valerie Glickman
illustrated by Chris Vallo

Decodable Story 18

Did you spot tracks in dirt at a pond? Which animal left them? That can be a puzzle at first.

Turtles live at ponds. Did you spot turtle tracks in that dirt?

On a pond's edge, birds and skunks look for turtle eggs. Did you spot bird or skunk tracks by eggshells?

A bobcat hunts after dark. Bobcat tracks can be hard to spot. Did you spot bobcat tracks?

Chipmunks run past ponds. Chipmunks live in long dirt tunnels. Bobcats can catch chipmunks. Did you spot chipmunk tracks?

Ducks paddle in ponds. Did you spot a duck's tracks? Kids walk at ponds. Did you spot more tracks?

Decodable Stories' Table

Getting Started

Lesson	Core Decodable	Practice Decodable	Sound/Spelling Correspondences	High-Frequency Words Introduced
Day 2	1 Sand, Tan Hats, and a Mat	1 Nat's Hats	/s/ spelled *s, ss* /m/ spelled *m* /t/ spelled *t, tt* /d/ spelled *d* /n/ spelled *n* /h/ spelled *h_* /a/ spelled *a*	give may these
Day 3	2 Hats!	2 Ants! Ants! Ants!	Review Day 2	
Day 4	3 Cass, Bill, and Mitt	3 Milt and Tam, a Tan Cat	/l/ spelled *l, ll* /b/ spelled *b* /k/ spelled *c* /i/ spelled *i*	
Day 5	4 Mitts and Hits	4 Ants at a Lamp	/k/ spelled *k* /p/ spelled *p* /r/ spelled *r* Review /i/	been our those
Day 6	5 A Big Fan	5 Grant Ran!	/f/ spelled *f, ff* /g/ spelled *g* /o/ spelled *o*	off
Day 7	6 A Best Pig Pin	6 Lists!	/j/ spelled *j* /ks/ spelled *x* /w/ spelled *w_* /e/ spelled *e, _ea_*	Mr. Mrs. read
Day 8	7 A Contest	7 Jeff and Max	Review /o/ /e/	stop tell who
Day 9	8 Gwen Must Run	8 Val's Van	/kw/ spelled *qu_* /v/ spelled *v* /y/ spelled *y_* /z/ spelled *z, zz, _s* /u/ spelled *u*	ten us
Day 10	9 Buzz, Buzz, Buzz	9 Gram's Land	Review consonants and short vowel sounds and spellings	

Unit 1

Lesson	Core Decodable	Practice Decodable	Sound/Spelling Correspondences	High-Frequency Words Introduced
Lesson 1	10 Chips	10 Finch Ranch	/ch/ spelled *ch* /th/ spelled *th* /sh/ spelled *sh*	far upon
	11 The Red Star	11 Bart's Farm Trip	/w/ spelled *wh_* /ar/ spelled *ar*	much start which
Lesson 2	12 A Bridge	12 Pudge Runs	/j/ spelled ■*dge* /k/ spelled ■*ck* /ch/ spelled ■*tch*	never under
Lesson 3	13 A Lunch List	13 Fluff	Review Unit 1 Lessons 1–2 Inflectional endings *-s, -es, -ed*	eight nine
Lesson 4	14 No Drinks in Class	14 Chuck's Shack	/ng/ spelled ■*ng* /nk/ spelled ■*nk* Inflectional ending *-ing*	bring thank think
	15 Paddle, Duck, Paddle	15 A Pink Gift	Schwa /ə/ spelled *el, le, al, il*	seven use why
Lesson 5	16 Learning to Swim	16 Pearl Helps Burt	/er/ spelled *er, ir, ur, ear*	better first learn
	17 Farm Chores	17 Mort on His Porch	/or/ spelled *or, ore*	animal black horse
Lesson 6	18 Tracks at a Pond	18 Turtle Shop	Review Unit 1	live

73

Grade 2 High-Frequency Words

again	easy	many	people	these
always	eight	may	picture	think
animal	everyone	mouse	piece	those
another	everything	Mr.	please	three
because	far	Mrs.	pull	today
been	few	much	quite	together
believe	first	myself	read	uncle
better	full	never	seven	under
black	give	new	show	upon
both	goes	nine	sign	us
bring	gray	off	small	use
brother	great	often	something	warm
brought	hold	once	soon	wash
buy	horse	only	sorry	which
carry	knew	open	start	white
center	laugh	other	stop	who
circle	learn	ought	taste	why
different	light	our	tell	work
does	listen	own	ten	write
done	live	paste	thank	zero

Grade 1 High-Frequency Words

about	come	how	one	too
after	could	if	or	two
an	day	into	over	very
any	don't	its	pretty	walk
are	every	jump	put	want
around	five	just	red	water
ask	four	know	ride	way
away	from	like	right	well
before	get	long	saw	went
big	going	make	six	where
blue	good	me	sleep	will
brown	got	my	take	would
by	green	no	their	yellow
call	help	now	them	yes
came	here	old	this	your

Grade K High-Frequency Words

a	did	her	on	they
all	do	him	out	to
am	down	his	said	up
and	for	I	see	was
as	girl	in	she	we
at	go	is	some	were
be	had	it	that	what
boy	has	little	the	when
but	have	look	then	with
can	he	of	there	you